The LITTLE INSTRUCTION BOOK for stude

Kate Freeman

summersdale

THE LITTLE INSTRUCTION BOOK FOR STUDENTS

Copyright © Summersdale Publishers Ltd, 2014

Research by Malcolm Croft

Illustrations by Kostiantyn Fedorov

Disclaimer
The advice in this book is purely for the purpose of entertainment and should not be followed.

Summersdale Publishers Ltd
46 West Street
Chichester
West Sussex
PO19 1RP
UK

www.summersdale.com

Printed and bound in the Czech Republic

ISBN: 978-1-84953-632-5

Substantial discounts on bulk quantities of Summersdale books are available to corporations, professional associations and other organisations. For details contact Nicky Douglas by telephone: +44 (0) 1243 756902, fax: +44 (0) 1243 786300 or email: nicky@summersdale.com.

To...... You...

From............. Me...

If we knew what it was we were doing, it would not be called research, would it?

Albert Einstein

Being a student is hard work, with long hours and little-to-no pay. And, despite universities having been around for over a thousand years, there is still no degree course anywhere in the world that teaches you how to be a great student – you have to just learn it on the job.

But, fret not, salvation lies inside!

The Little Instruction Book for Students is your indispensable bedside (and bar-side) companion to making the most of being a student, where – for the only time in your entire life – you'll enjoy lie-ins that last entire weekends, alcoholic drinks that cost less than a tin of baked beans and enough snogging to tire your tongue for the rest of your days. Enjoy!

Once your parents have dropped you off, they will have a deep desire to 'friend' you on Facebook to keep an eye on what you're doing. Create a pseudo account so they still think you're their innocent little angel.

When drunk, don't get a large kebab, large chips and fizzy soda. Get a small kebab, small chips and fizzy water.

Student loans are amazing. But don't blow the money all at once on unnecessary things, such as a motorbike, a £200 haircut and a whole new wardrobe of clothing.

Stay well clear from buying cleaning products from shops with names such as '£1 World', 'Cheapies' and 'Less4less'.

Come your second year you'll be used to living in your overdraft. Use these excuses when speaking to your local branch manager about why you need to extend your overdraft:

- 'I had to pay for flights for Ibiza during the summer. My, er, great-grandma's funeral was held there.'

- 'My landlord put my rent up... In fact, he's doubled it.'

- 'I give all my money to those charity workers on the streets.'

 Wear thick-rimmed glasses to make you look more intelligent.

Now you're all grown up, using emoticons and ungrammatical abbreviations is strictly forbidden.

Writing essays for a next-day deadline when you get back from the local nightclub is not to be encouraged. You may think that what you are writing is pure gold, but ultimately your 'sente4ncees luke a kot liKE Tthis bcos you haventhadthetime to speel chec4k tehm.'

Keeping pets, such as hamsters, gerbils or guinea pigs in your room on campus is not recommended. The temptation to pour wine in their water bottle 'to see if they get drunk like humans' is cruel.

If your mum and dad are paying for you to attend university, they will make you feel indebted to them. Ignore the following phrases that they will try to slip into conversation:

- 'Drinking every day? It's good to hear the money I'm paying for your education isn't being pissed up the wall.'

- 'If I'm going to pay for your textbooks, I expect you to look after them.'

- 'Your sister never caused this much trouble... She was a good girl.'

Most university campus bedrooms have a sink in them. Remember: *It is not a toilet.* It is a sink.

If you wee while having a shower, alert your roommate, especially if they're just about to have a bath.

Don't buy 'art' from Swedish-owned superstores.

Phone Roulette: the game that requires sending a naked picture of your intimate areas to a random person on your phone contact list. As long as 'Dan' receives the message, and not 'Dad', you'll be fine.

Before your first day at university, you'll feel the need to define yourself with a new hairstyle, or 'unique' sense of fashion. Try to resist this urge, as you'll only end up with a haircut you'll regret or a look that is the same as everyone else.

Jot down the university's major events in your diary the very minute you know of them. This will help you complete all coursework in advance of these dates.

Never buy new textbooks. Always, always, buy second-hand ones from former students or eBay. Here's why:

 You'll never read them.

 They're expensive if you're only going to use the paper as makeshift cigarette papers.

 All the information in them is on the Internet.

Students, as a rule of thumb, don't drink wine that costs more than £3.00 a bottle.

Never, ever, ever, utter the phrase, 'I'm never drinking again'. This is a lie.

When your place at university has been unconditionally offered (and you have accepted), locate the best pubs to go to, so that when you arrive you can impress your new friends with your knowledge of the area's best drinking and dining establishments.

Alarm clocks are important for students. But don't worry if you don't own one – you'll be woken up by 17 of your roommates at 8 a.m. every day, all asking if they can borrow a pen, laptop, money and/or clothing that is passably clean.

Never leave a floater in your shared toilet.

Three bits of advice you'll hear from your parents (most likely your dad) when they say goodbye after dropping you off that emotional first time. Heed their advice:

- 'Don't get anyone pregnant' / 'Don't get pregnant.'
- 'Try not to sleep with everybody.'
- 'Don't lend anybody any money – not even your friends. In fact, especially not your friends.'

Student nightclubs usually have the most cliched and ridiculous names. Avoid clubs with the names Tramps, Po Na Na and Sticky Fingers.

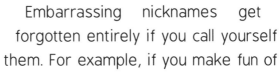

Embarrassing nicknames get forgotten entirely if you call yourself them. For example, if you make fun of yourself for having chlamydia, no one else will.

When introducing yourself to your classmates and professor in your first lecture, try your best to not piss-pronounce your murds.

Students will be students so, before you take up residence in your new room, thoroughly bleach the walls, steam-clean the carpets and wipe down every surface with industrial strength cleaner.

Three reasons not to sleep with anyone on the night before your first lecture:

- You don't want to be late and have to do the walk of shame across the lecture theatre.

- You'll be too tired to concentrate on the lecturer's dull voice.

- You might meet someone nicer on the second night.

When packing for university, leave your favourite teddy bear that you've had since you were born at home. Where it's safe.

If you're a science student, please refrain from using these chat-up lines:

- 'Billions of neutrinos penetrate you every second... Mind if I join in?'

- 'I wish I were adenine because then I could get paired with U.'

- 'Even if there wasn't gravity on earth, I'd still fall for you.'

Make sure you buy food in bulk and with an expiry date of 2150, such as dried pasta, packet noodles and a vat of rice.

 When drunk and full of 'Dutch courage' at 3 a.m. do not be tempted to call The Bank of Mum and Dad and ask to 'borrow more money, because you've spent your monthly allowance already'. Wait until sober.

Don't fall in love with the first boy / girl you meet just because they're new and different.

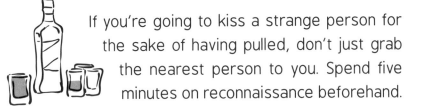

If you're going to kiss a strange person for the sake of having pulled, don't just grab the nearest person to you. Spend five minutes on reconnaissance beforehand.

Always buy teabags in the biggest box you can humanly carry. It's the only non-alcoholic drink you'll ever have from now on.

Keep baby wipes by your bedside. This'll help cool you down when you get the dreaded 'booze sweats'.

Sexually transmitted diseases may be very common, and proof that you've got lucky at least once, but, for everyone's sake, see a doctor.

After your first year of university, you'll probably be thrown off the university's campus and have to live off-site. When choosing a house, make sure:

- It's as close to campus as possible.
- Your mum and dad see it. They won't want you living in 'a nasty rat-infested bedsit'.
- There is enough space to play beer pong.

If you must decorate your new room with posters, resist the urge to include the ones with pretentious quotes. When you're in your room pissed-as-a-fart on alcopops and vomiting orange bile into a bucket, it's hard for anyone to take your beliefs seriously.

If you're going to trim your pubes in your shared shower, you can at least flush the offending hair away.

During your first night in the Student Union, resist the urge to put music on the jukebox. You don't want to be known as 'that Bryan Adams guy' for ever more.

Never quote any
philosophers at a party.

'Bake a quiche a week.' A motto every student should live by. One quiche slice contains your dairy, meat, vegetables and roughage all in one, and it lasts for ages!

Flirting with lecturers is only recommended if your professor looks more like Mr Schue than Dumbledore.

Printer jams, or printer meltdowns, when you have three seconds to hand in an important essay, are a severe pain in the bottom. Remain calm and do the following:

 Don't kick or punch the printer.

 Call up your dad – he'll know what to do.

 Don't waste time fixing yours, find a new one. Pronto.

'Borrowing' toilet rolls from campus is not encouraged, but everyone does it. You and your roommates should compete to see who can 'borrow' the most. Remember: every sheet helps.

'Reduced to Clear' – the three best words a student will read.

Many students (mainly male ones) feel the need to grow a beard, or worse, a little goatee, chin strap or moustache. If you're a man who can grow a thick beard, go nuts, but if you're still only able to grow peach fuzz, it's best to wait until you grow up properly.

Students are full of newly acquired wisdom. But they're also full of lies. Avoid the following gaffes when making your weekly phone call to your parents*:

THE LIE
'I go to all of my lectures.'

'I spend most of my time in the library.'

'I've met some really nice people.'

THE TRUTH
'I'm drunk right now.'

'I'm doing the bare minimum to pass.'

'I'm enjoying a lot of sex with strangers.'

*They won't believe a word of it.

Try to stay away from takeaways
that have the words 'perfect'
or 'cottage' in their name.

Don't post details of your house party on Facebook.

Nicknames can get out of hand at university. Your name might be Phil, but as a student – surrounded by a huge amount of new and different people – it'll magically turn into 'Philly P', 'the Phildog', 'P-money' and 'Philster'. Never call yourself by these names.

Condoms are provided free on campus during Freshers' Week. Don't be ashamed and/or embarrassed. Grab as many as you can.

If you're going to be sick (and you will be, constantly), then it's best to follow these ironclad instructions:

- 🎓 Throw up on yourself. It's easier to clean clothes than walls and carpets.

- 🎓 Never swallow your own sick. This only makes you want to throw up the sick you've just swallowed.

- 🎓 Never lift your head up to be sick. Drop your head, remain calm, and vomit slowly onto your chest.

 Students fall into several categories. Before you register on your first day, decide whether you will be The Nerd, The Booze Hound or The Promiscuous One.

Getting drunk at 9 a.m. is fun, but not if you miss your Summer Ball, which doesn't start until 7 p.m.

Student nightclub bouncers don't like it when you call them 'fat door openers'. You have been warned.

Embrace the traditions of a university student by drinking (or at least order) a Top Shelf – a mixture of the entire bar's spirits combined.

Students tend to cook the same cheap meal over and over again, i.e. potato waffles and baked beans. Most own brands have inexpensive ranges that cater for students, so don't be afraid to be more adventurous with your cooking.

Buy all the cheat sheets you can get your hands on.

If at all avoidable, don't use, or even own, a credit card. They're nothing but trouble.

Never be more than 15 minutes late for a lecture. Lecturers can be humorous people and will do their best to embarrass you for interrupting them, usually with the phrase 'I'm honoured that you graced us with your presence.'

Posting photos on Facebook, Twitter, Instagram, Snapchat, et al, while you're enjoying a night out may seem like a good idea at the time, but alcohol will seriously cloud your judgment. Don't post photos of the following nature:

-  Toilet selfies
-  Double chins
-  Weird eyes
- Bad hair
- Smeared make-up
- Inappropriate body parts

Date one of your uni's 'Ents' team. If you do, you'll never have to pay an entrance fee to an event ever again.

Student Unions like to hold social parties called 'Traffic Light Nights'. Always dress in green. You might not be single, but you can pilfer some free drinks out of people who fancy you.

Taking notes in lectures is a must. But don't bother bringing a pen along with you. Simply turn on the voice  memo app on your smartphone and record the lecturer speaking while you take a well-deserved nap.

If Facebook has taught us anything — it's date a computer student. One day they'll be rich.

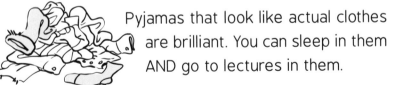

Pyjamas that look like actual clothes are brilliant. You can sleep in them AND go to lectures in them.

Cleaning the shared kitchen, especially doing the washing up, can become a monumental task. Be the one to employ a weekly rota, and give yourself the best shift – usually a Monday, as washing up tends to accumulate as the week goes on.

Never go for a number two at the Student Union loo. All the locks will be undoubtedly broken, and the seat will be made of cold metal.

Photocopying source books at the university library is expensive. And you have to wait your turn. Don't bother. Download a scanning app on your smartphone, or take pictures of the pages you need, and then print them out at home.

The best type of friend to make at university is the mature student. They're the ones that can help you out when you're in trouble. Here's why:

- They'll always have the textbooks/answers/a spare pad and pen during lectures.

- They're 97 per cent more likely to read the course material than you are.

- You'll make yourself seem cleverer, purely by association.

Make friends with somebody who doesn't drink. Pay for their soft drinks all night, on the condition that they make sure you get home safely.

If you're planning on going to a foam party, wear the worst and cheapest clothing you own. It's very difficult to get the smell of foam out of your clothes. And your skin.

If you're a girl, queuing for the loos on a night out is a problem. Quick fix: every time your boyfriend or male friend goes to the toilet, accompany him.

The worst type of friend to make at university is the Typical Student. They never listen, turn up to lectures in their pyjamas and never revise. Stay away from them – here's why:

- They'll doodle penises and boobs all over your notes during lectures.

- They rely on mature students to share their textbooks.

- They're always hungover and make terrible lecture partners.

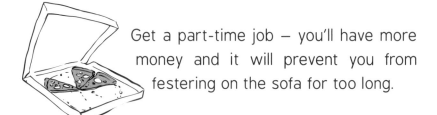

Get a part-time job – you'll have more money and it will prevent you from festering on the sofa for too long.

In order to pass the first year, develop a friendship with your lecturers. 'Bump' into them at any opportunity.

Halls of residence – the best place you'll ever live. Except when you forget to lock your door and all your friends burst in at the worst possible moment. ALWAYS LOCK YOUR DOOR.

Never play 'hide and seek' in your halls of residence. If you're drunk, you may fall asleep and wake up in a strange place.

Some students find it funny to play tricks on others. Beware of some of the non-food items that could surface in, or during, your meals:

 Blue plasters – fresh that day!

 Pubic hair, or hair of a non-pubic variety – not fresh that day!

 A fart – fresh or brewed, either will do!

Leave your posters of Ryan Gosling, Kelly Brook and *Star Wars* at home. Bring along some art from your mum and dad's house that they don't mind you 'borrowing'.

 Don't attend lectures without first breaking the spine of the textbook. Brand new and obviously unread books are the first thing lecturers tend to spot!

With the rise of social networks, it is a student's prerogative to 'friend', 'follow' and 'like' as many people as possible. Buck the trend.

When you know a lecturer will be marking your work, get their sympathy by saying your pet hamster died.

Embrace the time-honoured traditions of student life by stealing a traffic cone.

The best way to master drinking games is by building up a tolerance to alcohol by starting early.

A typical first-year student has between 10–20 hours of lectures a week. That leaves 150 hours or so to do as you please. In order to maximise the amount of fun to be had, the following is recommended:

🎓 Complete all coursework / revision during the day.

🎓 Get a good, sober night's sleep before all exams.

🎓 Pass your first year.

If you work part-time at a local office, 'borrow' the company's stationery and finish your essays during lunch (saves doing it when your shift finishes).

A big part of student life is playing Truth or Dare with your new buddies. Failure to play it will see you ostracised from the group. You must take part.

If you're in an exam and you need to write down a date you can't quite remember (was it 1897 or 1896?), try to fudge the answer by writing something that looks like a cross between the two.

Don't get a tattoo. After all, you will have to hide it from Mum and Dad once you're living back at home.

If you need a good excuse for being late to a lecture, the best will always be, 'Sorry, I was in bed with a naked boy / girl.' Your lecturer will understand and appreciate the honesty.

Losing your wallet or purse on a big night out is a student's rite of passage. Reduce the risk of losing anything important by leaving all your valuables at home.

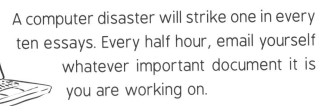

A computer disaster will strike one in every ten essays. Every half hour, email yourself whatever important document it is you are working on.

No self-respecting maths student should ever use the following chat-up lines. In fact, no one should use these chat-up lines, full stop.

 'I'm not being obtuse, but you're acute guy.'

 'You've got more curves than a triple integral.'

 'If you were sin^2x and I was cos^2x, then together we'd make one.'

If you're going to a house party, take your iPod and tell them to 'play some good music for a change'. Then put on some Chesney Hawkes.

Never high-five your professor at the end of an exam.

The only thing mums need is to know you are alright. Call, text or email your mum three times a week. If you don't do this – she'll come looking for you.

Take more photos of your friends being drunk than of yourself. In the morning when everyone is re-evaluating their behaviour from the night before, you'll have more proof than they do that they were more drunk than you were (even if this wasn't the case).

In an exam, DO NOT write 'YES' in the box marked 'SEX:'.